COYOTES

COYOTES

(Ki'yotes or Ki-yo'tays)

Written and Illustrated

by WILFRID S. BRONSON

SUNSTONE
PRESS

Sunstone books may be purchased for educational, business, or sales promotional use. For information please write: Special Markets Department, Sunstone Press, P.O. Box 2321, Santa Fe, New Mexico 87504-2321

Library of Congress Cataloging-in-Publication Data:

Bronson, Wilfrid S. (Wilfrid Swancourt), 1894-
  Coyotes / by Wilfrid Swancourt Bronson.
    p. cm.
  Originally published: New York : Harcourt, Brace, 1946.
  ISBN 978-0-86534-624-6 (softcover : alk. paper)
  1. Coyote–Juvenile literature. I. Title.

QL795.C6B7 2007
599.77'25–dc22

                    2007039731

Published in

WWW.SUNSTONEPRESS.COM
SUNSTONE PRESS / Post Office Box 2321 / Santa Fe. NM 87504-2321 /USA
(505) 988-4418 / orders only (800) 243-5644 / FAX (505) 988-1025

COYOTES

Gray Wolf : shoulders 28 inches high
weight 100 pounds

Coyote
21 inches
27 pounds

A wolf is a very wild kind of
dog. And a coyote is a small,
very smart kind of wolf. So a
coyote is a very smart kind of
wild dog.

Police Dog
24 inches
65 pounds

Red Fox
13 inches
10 pounds

A
COYOTE
is a fox-like wolf
with large ears
and a sharp
nose.

W. SB

A coyote does not want to live the way a tame dog does, with someone to feed him and give him a home. He wants to dig his own den and hunt his own supper.

But someone is always hunting
him, with guns or hounds or
traps or poison. He would be
much safer if he belonged to
someone. But a coyote only
wants to be his own dog, wild
and very free.

Thousands of years ago all dogs were wild. Our own ancestors were savages. Sometimes they stole wild woolly puppies from the wolves and raised them. These wild men's dogs were the ancestors of our tame dogs. People have changed since long ago, and so have dogs, but not the wolves and coyotes and foxes. Yet you can learn a lot about coyotes by looking at your dog.

Changes came in shape and size, hair and whiskers. Colors changed or came in spots and patches.

WSB

TUSKS FOR GRABBING AND HOLDING PREY ~ AND FOR SLASHING ENEMIES. SEE THE EMPTY SPACES ON THE GUMS WHERE THE TUSKS PASS EACH OTHER.

Grass-cutting and grain-grinding teeth of a Horse

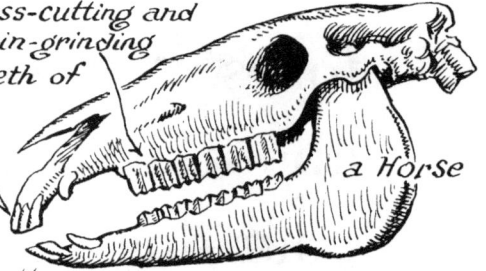

TEETH THAT JUST MEET, FOR HOLDING PREY AND FOR EASY CUTTING.

Small front teeth — for cleaning bits of meat from bones, currying out fleas,

SCISSOR TEETH THAT PASS EACH OTHER, CLOSE TO THE JAW MUSCLES, FOR CUTTING GRISTLE AND CRUNCHING BONES.

and cleaning caked snow or mud from paws.

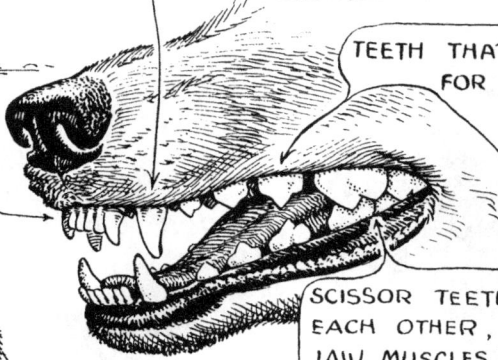

Look at the sharp pointed teeth. They belong to a hunting, meat-eating animal. There

DON COYOTE'S MENU

MICE ~ all Kinds
RATS ~ all Kinds
RABBITS ~ Jacks, Cottontails
GROUND-SQUIRRELS
PRAIRIE-DOGS
GOPHERS
GRASSHOPPERS
   CRICKETS
      JUNE-BUGS
DEAD ANIMALS
GARBAGE
STAGHORN "VELVET"
FROGS, SNAKES, LIZARDS
TURTLES, TURTLE EGGS
CRABS
FISH

SKUNKS ~~ WEASELS
GROUND-NESTING BIRDS
SHEEP (Shared with 100,000 stray and outlaw dogs)
DEER ~~ ANTELOPE
OTHER BIG GAME (Sick or wounded Elk, Moose, Bison, & Bighorn sheep)
CALVES & FAWNS (Of careless Mothers)
PIGLETS
POULTRY ~ Wild or tame

VEGETABLES
(Borrowed from Plant-eaters)
PEACHES, APRICOTS, PLUMS,
MELONS, GRAPES, ROSE-HIPS

[VEGETABLES CONTINUED ~~]
MESQUITE BEANS
CACTUS FRUIT
MANZANITA BERRIES
JUNIPER BERRIES

NOTE:
Because I eat whatever is offered, I can live where more particular animals would surely starve.
Signed,
Don Coyote

are no broad teeth growing close together for grinding grain and greens, like a plant-eating animal's. The jaws cannot swing sideways even a little to do such grinding. A meat-eater simply catches a plant-eater, chops it up, and swallows it in hunks and chunks.

Look at the claws. On tough springy legs the coyote bounces easily along. His stout claws dig into the ground like runing-spikes. His foreclaws will hold a field mouse underneath the grass till he can take it in his teeth. They are his tools when he digs out gophers and such prey, or digs a den, or buries food to save it. The hind claws are good scratchers when he itches underneath his fur.

5 Claws

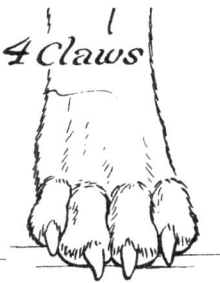

4 Claws

FRONT PAW   HIND PAW

WSB

A good thing I always wear my overcoat and wool under~clothes!

THE ORIGINAL MUFF

The coyote has two kinds of fur: soft wool close to his body, and longer hair which grows out through it. The wool keeps his body warm and the hair sheds rain and keeps it dry. His coat is thicker in winter and so, though food is often scarce, he may not look too thin. A coyote's tail makes a warm muff for his naked nose and toes when sleeping in cold weather.

It is tipped with black, but most of his fur is a mixture of yellow and gray. With brown tints on the short hair of his face and legs he is altogether like the dusty earth and half-dried grasses of the prairie. Thus he can almost vanish just by holding still.

This is very useful to a hunting and a hunted animal.

His black-lidded eyes are am-
ber. They glow greenish-gold
in the night. They are very

Part of my wild
look lies in the
slant of my eyes.

good eyes. But, like other dogs,
a coyote reads mostly with his
keen, wet nose. With a sniff he
reads the air and can tell if
friends or enemies are near, or
where his supper may be wait-
ing. Or, sniffing the ground, he
may read which way his supper
has been traveling, and follow
and catch up with it.

By sniffing special stumps and clumps, he can read the latest "Dog-World News." He learns of every other coyote or wolf or dog that has come along his favorite trails, if it was male or female, old or young, well or ill, happy or worried. For each one,

Each one's scent varies with his condition.

first reading "the latest," also leaves his own sign there before going on. Some also scratch the ground with all four feet, as though drawing firm lines under

their names to make them look more bold. And a coyote carefully sniffs a strange coyote, reading his character to find out if he cares to be a friend. Coyotes are the most musical

ONE COYOTE
SINGING

Some say
he really
yodels
too~

yip yip yipe!

yaroo oooo!

yiper cooer ooo! oo!

yap! yap yap

yep?

of all dogs, wild or tame. A wolf howls. A tame dog barks and sometimes howls. But sometimes a coyote seems to bark and howl and sing bass to his own tenor all at the same time. To human ears one coyote sounds like a whole quartette

gone crazy. But to the coyote it is a lovely noise, and his sharp ears hear even more of it than ours do. He may sing just for the sake of it. But often he is sending messages across the prairie: "Look out, brothers; I smell a gun-man!" Or "Come, friends. Good hunting here!" Often just at sunset he may serenade his wife.

We can call her that because coyotes mate for life. They stand by and help each other year after year, through good times and bad. Like our tame dogs, coyotes have very loyal natures. But being wild, and loving no human master, they give this deep devotion to their mates. Tonight perhaps the coy-

ote pair is planning lamb for

supper. When a settler comes, with his cows and sheep, into wild new country to start a ranch or farm, he tries to kill all the coyotes. This is very hard to do, for some coyotes always understand his tricks and have many of their own. They will not eat his poison; they spring his traps, and keep just too far off for him to shoot them. But meanwhile the settler is busily killing off their natural food. He shoots the deer and antelope and poisons as many rabbits, ground-squirrels, rats, mice,

and grasshoppers as he can. All these creatures eat of the grass he wants for his sheep and cattle. So once in a while, in spite of his gun and great fierce dogs, he has to pay a little rent to the coyotes whose land he uses. Though he has destroyed

THE SETTLER'S FOOD SUPPLY PLUS ALL THE ANIMALS HE RAISES FOR THE MARKET.

BALANCE BETWEEN

most of their natural food, they still must eat; so they collect a calf or sheep or chicken or turkey when they get a chance. Somehow this seems only fair.

Often a settler tries to raise
too many sheep and cattle.
There is not grass enough to go
around. His animals never get
enough to eat. And so, on cold
winter nights out on the range,
the weaker ones lie down and
die. This is lucky for the coyotes.
They are half starved themselves. They cannot dig out any
prairie-dogs or rats and mice
sleeping in the hard frozen

ground, so they clean every scrap from the bones of dead cows or sheep or horses. If the settler sees their tracks in the snow about the skeletons he thinks the coyotes killed his animals. But he himself has really done it by having more on the range than it can feed. The coyotes do him a service, cleaning up the carcasses before they spoil the streams when the

snow begins to melt. Coyotes also take away many dead creatures killed on the highways by automobiles. They often clean up garbage left in lovely places by bad-mannered picnickers. Many people have called the coyote a villain and a coward. But to the coyote it is not wrong to take a supper now and then from men who take his natural prey from him and would take

He goes where he sees the soaring buzzard diving toward the earth. There, possibly, is food that he can claim.

his life too if they could. A hunting animal is not cowardly because he uses tricks, lying in ambush or sneaking up on his prey. How else can he catch anything? Even human hunters use every trick that they can

Here the "sneak attack" is being used by both hunters.

think of. A coyote is a fierce
fighter and generally can whip
a single dog of his own size or
bigger. But it is not cowardly to
run from a whole pack of dogs

with armed men behind them on horses or in roaring automobiles. It is just good sense. How long could he live if he

didn't run? Coyotes use many tricks in order to catch their prey, to take food from the settler, and to save themselves from the hunter and his dogs.

A FEW COYOTE WAYS

1 **TO HUNT PRAIRIE-DOGS ALONE ~**
(Be sure the wind blows toward you, not the prairie-dog.)

1

Slink forward when the prey lowers its head to crop grass.
(With its head in the grass it cannot see you.)

2

Be still as a stone when it sits up to chew.
(It doesn't notice things that do not move.)

3

Spring for the catch when it is cropping grass again.

3 **TO HUNT GROUND~SQUIRRELS WITH A BADGER ~**
(The Badger didn't invite you, but) look for a back door to the squirrel's

② TO HUNT PRAIRIE-DOGS WITH ANOTHER COYOTE ~

(Prairie-dogs cannot count, even up to 2.)

1

Let **X** follow **Y** right up to the edge of the prairie-dog town.
Let **Y** keep going. Let **X** crouch, very still.

2

Soon the prairie-dogs will peek out of their holes. But they will notice only **Y**
who is <u>moving away</u>.

3

Let **X** make the catch while all prairie-dogs are barking bad names at **Y**.

...est. You can snatch any   squirrels which try to leave that way, the
                                                       ones the badger
                                                         is sure to
                                                            miss.

4 TO RUN DOWN AN ANTELOPE (or Deer or Jack-rabbit) →

This circle is really a mile or so   across...

you never can keep up with an antelope, but you can chase it in a -------

SOME WAYS OF KEEPING

1 A RELAY TO SAVE YOUR MATE FROM GREYHOUNDS AND...

YOU HIDE AND START FROM HERE.

You had better invite other coyotes to help you, for

----wide circle and tire it out by running in relays, yourselves.

COYOTES ALIVE

----WOLFHOUNDS~

When she begins to tire, cut across her path just ahead of the dogs. They will follow you. Starting fresh, perhaps you can wear them out. If not, having rested, your mate can take another turn at leading them, and so on. Thus, working together, you may spoil their hunting and save your lives.

2 *The hounds are bigger than you are. Maybe you can slip through and pile them up at a barbed wire fence.*

3

At least once, jumping onto a speeding flat-car saved a coyote's life.

4 *Of course men follow dogs. If you know of an old den that has two doors, lead them to the front door, then slip out the back and leave your enemies digging you out after you are already miles away.*

I HAD TO MOVE OUT OF THIS DEN LAST SUMMER, IT GOT SO FULL OF FLEAS. BUT IT COMES IN HANDY TODAY!

WAYS OF COLLECTING

Draw off the slow farm dogs and shepherd while your mate, un—noticed, quietly carries off a lamb.

Turkeys (wild or tame) can be had from am—bush, especially if their minds are all on catching grasshoppers.

FROM THE SETTLER

To pick up a piglet,
make a bold commando
dash right into the barn~
yard and out again before
they can gather their wits.

February is the month of brides for coyotes. Then all unmarried female coyotes that have reached two years of age find husbands. Several males may fight for a single female, but finally when she chooses one of them, the others all give up like gentlemen. She doesn't always take

The
Tournament

the one who fought the best. It
may be the one who got the very
worst of it. Maybe she thinks he
will stand by her best in trouble-
some times and endure the most
for her sake. Maybe she is flat-
tered by the wounds he bears
for her. Anyway, from then on
and for the rest of their lives,
they are

Mr. and Mrs. Coyote.

There is a kind of honeymoon
time when they do everything
together. They hunt together,
play together, rest together, and
just enjoy each other's company,
with never a thought of anyone

else. But soon the female does have thoughts of others. She begins to look for a good place to dig a den where she can have her puppies. Some spot on a hillside facing south, with bushes to

"zzz-what I don't know won't hurt me-zz"

A FEAST FOR TWO

hide the entrance, would suit her
perfectly. She may start to dig
in such a spot. Or perhaps there
is an old badger or a ground-hog
hole already there. This is good
luck, for she needs only to en-

large it. The male takes his turn with the work, and if they are enlarging a ground-hog's hole, they may dig him out, still in his winter sleep, and have a feast without his ever waking up to know about it.

A PLAN of the COYOTE'S DEN

Sometimes they tunnel out a back door also.

Backing out with Dug Dirt

Dug Dirt ↘

WSB

Every day between hunting trips, some digging is done, not hurrying, just getting ready in plenty of time. They hollow out a room at the tunnel's end. Then they dig up to the surface of the ground to make a small hole for

Pack-rat's Tunnel

Digging to make a Ventilator

a ventilator. Sometimes it is only necessary to dig into a gopher hole or pack-rat's tunnel which leads up to the air. Finally they may bring in a little dry grass and bark for bedding, though this is not always done.

If you could see inside the nursery

The big birthday comes in April. With their eyes still closed, five to ten dark gray puppies whimper feebly but struggle strongly, each for its share of mother's milk. Already each is learning to look out for itself.

This is well, for the world is a difficult and dangerous place for coyotes. Smacking loudly, they suckle till their little bellies bulge, and then they sleep. Except to drink, the mother does not leave them for the first two days or so. And the father, hunting alone and twice as hard as usual, brings food for her to the doorway of the den.

(Not far from the mother's den, the father digs himself a sleeping den. There the puppies can be taken quickly if the nursery is discovered by a man.)

After nine days the puppies' eyes come open, but they see very little, deep in the darkness of the den. When they are about three weeks old, the mother brings them out for a toddle-frolic in the sun about the door. She does this every day. At first they play with their own toes and tails, then with their brothers' and sisters'. Walking is a hard thing to learn, and at first they can knock themselves down just by trying to bark. But as the days pass they even learn to run, stumbling and

sprawling at first but soon romp-
ing all about. They play hide-
and-jump-out, and they wrestle
hard. It is just like the play of
tame puppies, but for coyote
puppies it is also practice for the
hunting and fighting they will
have to do when they are older.

Mother is weaning them now, not on raw meat, but on meat cooked in her own stomach. She can unswallow just as smoothly as she swallows. So when she catches a jack-rabbit she eats it, and by the time she gets home it is "tenderized" enough for little puppies. If the mother is

killed, the father coyote will feed his babies this way till they can eat the game he brings just as he caught it.

The hungry puppies may see their parents a long way off and even smell what they are bringing home for dinner. But it is against the rules to run to meet

them. They must not go more than about fifty feet from the doorway of the den. A coyote puppy that goes wandering off on a walk may be seen by men who will chase him home and thus discover the den. Then they are sure to dig all the puppies out and kill them. Or an eagle or horned-owl or mountain lion might carry off the wayward puppy to feed to its own wild young ones. Any coyote pup that goes beyond the safety zone gets a severe nipping from his angry mother and he doesn't

do it any more.

But by July the puppies are half grown and can go on their first hunting trip with their parents. Maybe they catch only

A FIRST LESSON IN MOUSING: Pounce where the
You should snatch by the back of the neck

This is going to be easy!

Ah! Got him!

A NEW DELIGHT --
Lapping Water

crickets and grasshoppers that
first day. But they go every day
and, watching the old ones, soon
learn to catch mice. By Septem-

grass is wiggling. But remember,~ mice can bite too!
and give one quick shake.

Ow!
Wow!

EEK!

ber they are helping to run down rabbits and other good-sized game. Now the mother shows them traps and poisoned bait and lets them scent the smells of man, at the same time snarling and nipping them away from all such things. Some of the puppies will not learn from this teaching. They will be caught

Odors of the terrible Man-Animal who can kill from a distance.

Springing a TRAP

BUT SOME MUST LEARN THE HARD WAY.

or, at best, leave several toes in traps, before they understand. But always one or two are extra bright. They may live close to the settler for years and raise their own pups there, in spite of all he can do to drive them off or kill them. Coyotes are so intelligent that Indians have always believed that they are gods in disguise, or that when an Indian dies he turns into a coyote. Indians therefore have

Tales of the
Superdog

never been willing to kill coyotes. But white men have been killing coyotes for over three hundred years. Spanish settlers

began about 1600. Before the
white men came, the coyotes all
lived west of the Mississippi
River and south of Canada. Yet
now these little wolves (which
never attack human beings)
have spread into several states
east of the Mississippi, and clear
up into Alaska. Some very clever
ones have even raised their puppies right in city suburbs. So
perhaps those footprints you
saw in the new concrete side-
walks on the edge of town were

not made by some tame old towser, but are the tracks of a real live coyote, your very wild new next-door neighbor.

The End

www.ingramcontent.com/pod-product-compliance
Lightning Source LLC
Chambersburg PA
CBHW081240090426
42738CB00016B/3358